TABLE OF CONTENT

Why You Lie, Cheat & Deceive
The Eleventh Book in the "Why" Series of Books
©Copyright 2013 by Dr. Leland Benton

DISCLAIMER AND TERMS OF USE AGREEMENT:

(Please Read This Before Using This Book)

This information is for educational and informational purposes only. The content is not intended to be a substitute for any professional advice, diagnosis, or treatment.

The author and publisher of this book and the accompanying materials have used their best efforts in preparing this book.

The author and publisher make no representation or warranties with respect to the accuracy, applicability, fitness, or completeness of the contents of this book. The information contained in this book is strictly for educational purposes. Therefore, if you wish to apply ideas contained in this book, you are taking full responsibility for your actions.

The author and publisher disclaim any warranties (express or implied), merchantability, or fitness for any particular purpose. The author and publisher shall in no event be held liable to any party for any direct, indirect, punitive, special, incidental or other consequential damages arising directly or indirectly from any use of this material, which is provided "as is", and without warranties. As always, the advice of a competent legal, tax, accounting, medical or other professional should be sought where applicable.

The author and publisher do not warrant the performance, effectiveness or applicability of any sites listed or linked to in this book. All links are for information purposes only and are not warranted for content, accuracy or any other implied or explicit purpose. No part of this may be copied, or changed in any format, or used in any way other than what is outlined within this course under any circumstances. Violators will be prosecuted.

One of the most perplexing human conditions is why people find a need to lie, cheat and deceive. Deception has become a lifestyle and more people spend their lives within a web of deception than outside of it. They have built whole worlds within their existences and many have no idea how it occurred or how to stop it.

In this book, I want to address the subject of lies, cheats and deception in detail and I am quite certain you will be amazed. One would think that les, cheating and deception are really one-in-the-same but they are not and like I said, you will be amazed at just how distinct the reasons behind all three really are and how compelling they are to break.

In the book, "Man Up-The Decline & Fall of Manhood" Dr. Noah Pranksky defines the decline of manhood with the main cause being deception.

http://www.amazon.com/dp/B006JA2UMG

Furthermore, in another of his books, "Female Wolf Packs" he demonstrates the problems men have with women and the leading problem is deception.

http://www.amazon.com/dp/B006JMHD80

The problem of "trust' between genders has become so severe that each gender is literally giving up on relationships and going off to form family units without the opposite gender in the picture. Women are using the services of sperm banks to sire children and men are choosing surrogate mothers.

The question of "why" has been a part of the conscience of man since the dawn of time. It has caused us to seek answers, better solutions, invention, progress, increased knowledge and more.

But more often than not, most of our questions of "why" now centers on personal behavioral traits and habits that perplex us and cause us consternation and regret.

Candidly, most people have no idea why they do the things they do so in this book – the eleventh book in the "Why" series of books – I am going to explain in detail why you lie, cheat and deceive and how to overcome these perplexing problems.

The subsequent books in this series will deal with specific behavioral traits and target certain conditions that really are bothersome. To wit:

Why you Do The Things You Do
Why You Are Greedy
Why You Are Immoral
Why You Are In Debt Up To Your Eyeballs
Why You Are Lonely
Why You Are Unhappy
Why You Fail In Relationships
Why You Get Angry
Why You Gossip About Others
Why You Have Bad Habits
Why You Lie, Cheat & Deceive
Why You Overeat
Why You Procrastinate
Why You Smoke

In all of the books of this "Why" series, Chapter 1 always begins with "Laying a Proper Foundation" and deals with the mechanism of the human mind and how the mind functions both conscious mind and subconscious mind. This is a very important chapter so please study this chapter closely.

I will then teach you how to change the subconscious mind's belief systems. In other words, the Introduction and Chapter 1 will appear in the entire "Why" series of books as the foundation. From Chapter 2 on, I will then discuss each book's specific topic in detail.

It is important to note that there is no such thing as "personal" versus "commercial" behavioral science. The human mind uses the same mechanism in both personal situations as well as commercial.

The way each individual/gender employs their respective psyches is what is different.

For example; we all have cars but we all have different driving habits and drive cars differently.

Hence, in a personal situation, i. e. relationships or a commercial situation, i.e. addicted to shopping, the human mind employs the same mechanism and the corrective protocols used to correct any of the situations described in the "Why" series of books will be similar.

So let's get to it…

Chapter 1 - Laying A Proper Foundation

In all of my "Why" series of books, I will provide the following discourse on the Human Mind in order to lay a proper foundation to what I am about to teach.

The Mechanism of the Human Mind

Which Comes First - the Body or the Mind?
(the most important concept in all of talk therapy)

Understanding the Body - Mind Connection

For thousands of years, we have known there is a body – mind connection. Until now though, we have not known what this connection is. What it it? Time. The body and the mind each have their own sense of time. Their own clocks so to speak. Therapy works only when these two clocks are in sync.

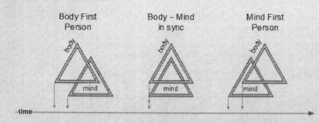

Body First Person   Body – Mind in sync   Mind First Person

9

Prior to the fall of man into sin as described in the Garden of Eden, man's spirit was hooked to God's infinite spirit. There was no death because God's spirit is infinite. Man is the only animal on earth that shares the eternality nature of God. The subject of eternal life has been a heated topic of man from the beginning of our existence.

In Greek mythology, there's a story about a mortal youth named Tithonus. Aurora, the goddess of dawn, fell in love with the boy and when Zeus, the king of the gods, promised to grant Aurora any gift she chose for her lover, she asked that Tithonus might live forever. But, in her haste she forgot to ask for eternal youth, so when Zeus granted her request, Tithonus was doomed to an eternity of perpetual aging as a grouchy old man... forever.

In the movie "Highlander," Angus McLeod was born in 1518 as an immortal being. He could not die and to me, the best part of the movie was the depiction of this immortal's agony here on earth as he watched everything he loved die forcing him to begin his life over and over again. He saw all of the ugliness, which man had caused over four centuries. He witnessed the Spanish Inquisition, Waterloo, the atrocities of the Third Reich, and more. He saw the slavery and bigotry of the eighteenth century, the slaughter of the Native American tribes after the Civil War. This man's life was a living Hell!

There is a very big difference between the ways our feeble minds picture eternal life versus God's idea of eternal life. Our understanding comes from Quantum Physics and is limited within the Time-Space Continuum.

Life is your spirit, but the soul of man has usurped the spirit's position and psychology is now forced to define "how" we live our lives based on the animating force of the soul instead of the spirit. As I said previously, the soul has usurped the spirit's place as our animating force. Let's discuss this now.

❖ **Body First Person** - When the body becomes our life, we live as animals.
❖ **Body-Mind In Sync** - When the soul becomes our life, we live as rebels and fugitives in a life of desires, emotions, and will (consuming entities). This is the position of mankind today!
❖ **Mind First Person** - But when we come to live our life in the mind/spirit and by the spirit, though we still use our soul's faculties just as we do our physical faculties, they are now the servants of the spirit.

If you live as a consuming entity, you will always lose. In other words, to get, you must give - you must sacrifice! Have you ever wondered why you have so many anxieties, phobias, worries and fears? The reality of this world is evil. So what is reality? I will tell you. This is reality:

"Life without war is impossible either in nature or in grace. The basis of physical, mental, moral and spiritual life is antagonism. Health is the balance between physical life and external nature, and it is maintained only by sufficient vitality on the inside against things on the outside. Everything outside my physical life is designed to put me to death. Things, which keep me going when I

11

am alive, disintegrate me when I am dead. If I have enough fighting power, I produce the balance of health.

The same is true of mental life. If I want to maintain a vigorous mental life, I have to fight, and in that way the mental balance called thought is produced. Morally it is the same. Everything that does not partake of the nature of virtue is the enemy of virtue in me, and it depends on what moral caliber I have whether I overcome and produce virtue (GOOD CHARACTER). Immediately I fight, I am moral in that particular. No man is virtuous because he cannot help it; virtue (character) is acquired.

- ❖ Psychology only studies the observable aspects of the mind and discounts the unseen or intangible aspects of the human mind.
- ❖ Behavioral science attempts to study the intangible aspects of the human mind…why you do the things you do and more importantly why you don't do what you should do.
- ❖ There is no such thing as commercial psychology versus personal psychology. The mind uses the same mechanism to evaluate all types of relationships.
- ❖ Everything we do revolves around relationships. We relate to our environment, our friends, family, co-workers, other people and even our pets. We are social animals.

The Mechanism of the Human Mind

Belief Systems + Thought + Delight = Action/Behavior/Conduct

Conscious Mind

5-senses:
Sight
Hearing
Taste
Touch
Smell
ESP (women only)

Subconscious Mind

Intellect:
Experiential
Empirical

DEW:
Desires, Emotions and Will

The Human Psyche Differences Between Genders

The female psyche operates on emotional, spiritual, physical and intellectual planes
The male psyche operates only on the intellectual and physical planes.

Here is an exercise you might find weird but it demonstrates the power of the human mind.

Fi yuo cna raed tihs, yuo hvae a sgtrane mnid too. Cna yuo raed tihs? Olny 55 plepoe out of 100 can. I cdnuolt blveiee taht I cluod aulaclty uesdnatnrd waht I was rdanieg. The phaonmneal pweor of the hmuan

13

mnid, aoccdrnig to a rscheearch at Cmabrigde Uinervtisy, it dseno't mtaetr in waht oerdr the ltteres in a wrod are, the olny iproamtnt tihng is taht the frsit and lsat ltteer be in the rghit pclae. The rset can be a taotl mses and you can sitll raed it whotuit a pboerlm. Tihs is bcuseae the huamn mnid deos not raed ervey lteter by istlef, but the wrod as a wlohe. Azanmig huh? Yaeh and I awlyas tghuhot slpeling was ipmorantt!

You might have found it somewhat unusual that you could probably read the jumbled mess above. Actually over half the people that see this exercise can decipher the words at the same speed of reading as if the words were not jumbled.

It is important to note that the human mind thinks in packages…concepts rather than individual ideas.

Your eyes see each letter but the mind looks at the whole word instead. As you read, the mind looks at the first and last letter only. Remember this; the mind sees the beginning and end. We will talk about this later…

If you were to listen to an orchestra, your ear listens to every note from every instrument but a trained ear can actually pick out individual instruments from the whole sound as the mind hears the whole symphony.

How does this apply to you?

Learning to observe means going beyond the mind's natural ability to only read the first and last letters of a word!

It is training the mind to see all the letters, not just the eye but the mind!

Truisms About the Human Mind

❖ Pain vs. Pleasure – people are more motivated to avoid pain than seek pleasure.
❖ A person that is suffering depression will seek relief (notice I didn't say cure) before they seek happiness.
❖ The human mind cannot tell the difference between fantasy and reality.
❖ The human mind gravitates to the desires, emotions and will of its psyche. People crave entertainment so fantasy dominates their existences.
❖ The human mind is easily distracted! You can either be the cause of these distractions or other stimuli will be the cause but rest assured people WILL BE distracted because the human mind is gullible.

The human mind responds quickly to these three forms of stimuli

❖ Sex
❖ Humor
❖ FEAR

But the greatest of them all is FEAR!

BTW – on the positive side we have faith, hope, love, but the greatest of these *is* LOVE.

Fear usually takes the form of what is called "Scarcity Thought"

You are afraid that someone will have what you feel belongs to you or that others will have more "stuff" than you.

❖ The subconscious mind is often referred to as the "heart," and is the control mechanism the body uses to store our beliefs.

❖ **These beliefs are stored as pictures in our "hearts" and create frequencies in our bodies.**

❖ We know that the optimum human frequency is a little below 7.83 hertz. To drop below this frequency brings on the onslaught of disease. To rise above it a person demonstrates psychic abilities.

❖ Harmful beliefs that cause unhealthy frequencies are the source of almost all problems - physical, mental, emotional.

❖ The subconscious mind creates a belief system, which we call "pictures of the heart."

❖ These pictures involve either visions, or dreams/fantasies.

❖ Science has discovered that the subconscious mind cannot distinguish between fantasy and reality.

*The subject of all dreams is the dreamer.
*Dreams are born in our desires, emotions and will.
*Dreamers believe in a belief system, which is fantasy.
*A life lived within a fantasy creates a feeling of self-centeredness, hopelessness and despair. In dreams everything is perfect.
*The subject of a vision is not the visionary but the world.
*Visions are born in the intellect.
*Visions are pictures of the future that have already been experienced in the heart of those who give it birth.
*Visionaries sacrifice themselves for the good of mankind.
*Visions have a moral quality that transcends the self-centered nature of dreams.
*By its very nature a vision launches a mission, a "cause-that-inspires."
*Visions create a sense of belonging.

❖ We act upon visions and/or dreams, using thought.
❖ Thought employs the intellect, in the case of visions, or the desires, emotions and the will, in the case of dreams.
❖ Intellectual thought relies on wisdom; emotional thought relies on the pursuit of pleasure, comfort and delight.
❖ Dreamers live within a facade; they create a false sense of worth using imaginary situations.

- ❖ Visionaries live within reality; they create change, within a framework of restraint, and intellectual thought.
- ❖ The world is made up of OPPOSITES, which is usually the corrupted version of the original. We have good and evil. We have love and lust!
- ❖ EVERYTHING YOU DO IS BECAUSE OF LOVE OR LUST. Learn to love because there are no crimes beyond forgiveness.

*Love is born in the intellect; lust is born in the DEW!
*Love is vision; lust is fantasy.
*Love restrains & sacrifices; lust is selfish
*Love is being one with someone or something
*Lust is being with someone or something.
*Visionaries love; dreamers lust!
*Visionaries do what is required; dreamers just do their best!

WHEN THERE IS NO HOPE OF LOVE DO WE ABANDON OURSELVES TO LUST?

Yes we do!

Pictures of the heart are your belief system.

- ❖ We animate these pictures into either fantasies, or visions.
- ❖ People do not appear to see the difference between the matter part of an organism and the life part, which animates it.

18

- We seem to think that the organism itself is life. In other words, it is not our outward appearance that is our life, but our inward existence.
- Life is what goes into the body. Death is what comes out.
- A person who lies is not a liar because he tells a lie. The lie is the manifested behavior of some subconscious belief system. The lie only demonstrates that the person is a liar…it is the effect.
- Except for love, the power of words inspired by a vision or fantasy is the most potent human force.

"Do you want to have or do you want to be?"

*For a dreamer: "Seeing is believing!"
*But they only see imaginary things that are not real!!
*This is why "The Secret" is WRONG!
*Say it and claim it is WRONG!
*Blab it and grab it IS WRONG!
*See it and be it IS WRONG!
Dreamers practice companionship – To be with someone or something!

VERY IMPORTANT:

1. Dreamers covet the object of their temptation, BUT they covet the temptation more so than the object itself because the temptation is the idol of their fantasy.
2. If there is a conflict between the conscious and subconscious mind, the subconscious mind always wins…ALWAYS!

3. All reaction occurs in the conscious mind; all interaction occurs in the subconscious mind. Fear is a "REACTION" to losing control.

For a visionary: "Believing is seeing!"

There are no SECRETS; there are only challenges to be conquered!

THIS IS NOT A SECRET: Putting a photo of a Ferrari on your refrigerator and seeing yourself driving it by employing the so-called law of attraction is pure BUPKES!!! Why? Because this is all occurring in the conscious mind and beliefs reside in the subconscious mind. How do you transfer something from the conscious mind to the subconscious mind and make it a belief system?

A Ferrari is the object of your temptation but what you covet most is the temptation of owning a Ferrari because the temptation is the idol of your fantasy.

It is all about ATTENTION & ACCEPTANCE!!!!! I have a $100 bill in my hand and I am willing to give it to you. But if you don't ACCEPT it then it is still in my hand. BELIEF SYSTEMS ARE CREATED BY ATTENTION & ACCEPTANCE!

John 1:12 But as many as received him, to them gave he **the right** to become children of God, *even* to them that believe on his name

Human things must be known to be loved; but divine things must be loved to be known.

BELIEVING IS SEEING!

Let's talk about goals…which of the following goals are good goals?

❖ To want to get married and have a wonderful, happy, loving marriage?
❖ To want to have children who are happy, successful, and loving?
❖ To have a successful, fulfilling and rewarding career?
❖ Is it a good goal to want to have fun, bonded, loving, and meaningful relationships with other people?

Which of the listed goals are good goals? None of them!

You should never have anything for a goal that is not 100% under your control, AND each and every goal should be <u>motivated by love</u>.

Almost all goals that we have in our life are wrong.

Everything that we do, we do because of a goal we have.

When we get up in the morning, it's because of some goal that we have; we are hungry for breakfast, or we need to go to work.

If we go to the grocery store, it's because of some goal we have. If we are kind to people, it's because of some goal that we have.

Now we don't always know what they are, because a lot of these are subconscious goals.

The goals we have are the reasons for everything we do. But, do all of your goals involve only YOU?

Of course not!

And when the other person, or persons, in your goal do not perform, or act the way you want them to, then we become anxious and stressed.

When our goals get blocked, it creates anger, anxiety, and frustration. If we only have good goals, we will not experience anger or anxiety.

That's how you know, if you are living a wrongful goal. If the result is anger and frustration because your control was blocked and blocking your goal, then you had a wrongful goal. It may have been a fine and noble desire, but a wrongful goal.

Filters

We live in a society of consumerism and entertainment. In my previous books I have spoken reams about this subject. Instant gratification is paramount and today's technology delivers information and other stimuli in bucketfuls to the human mind. We have already spoken about filters that the human mind employs to weed out what it determines to be irrelevant. This "irrelevancy" is different in every individual and many times is programmed into our minds subconsciously or without us knowing it. We have also spoken about the causes of these various filters such as environment, maturity, upbringing, culture, etc.

The one essential common element of all filters is that they are all ATTENTION diverters. We have spoken about attention earlier; what is very interesting is that filters are generally viewed as bad when some are really very good.

I had a friend, who lives in Chicago, fall on hard times and needed assistance. When I got to him he was living in a cheap hotel and had a room so small when you put the key in the door you broke the *window (I slay me)*. His room was about 50 feet from the Loop (the overhead train that circles around Chicago). The noise was deafening when the train went by, and it went by often, but my friend had filtered it out. Amazing, but when you thing about it, my friend really does hear the train but yet he pays no attention to it, so in actuality, it is like he doesn't hear it at all! So filters divert attention, and take away our focus; so let's talk about focus.

The Incredible Power of Focus

One of the more important points I have made has been the idea that you really do create your own life and your own reality. I know this idea has become a kind of personal growth cliché that many of us have heard over and over for years. Many people, after continuing to experience the same old ups and downs and personal dramas over many years, get to the point where they dismiss this idea as charming but useless -- or just plain wrong. "If I'm creating this, then I'm certainly not doing it on purpose," they say. "It sure seems like this is HAPPENING to me, rather than that I'm creating it." They just assume that it's all BS because "this and this and this and this are going on for me, and I have no control over it, and anyone who thinks I'm creating this doesn't understand what I'm going through." Essentially, they are resigning themselves to becoming a victim of circumstances.

We live in a universe of infinite complexity and many forces -- way too many to keep track of -- operate on us. Yes, it is true that we are NOT in control of everything that happens, because we are not in control of most of those infinite other parts of the universe. In fact, the only thing you have total and complete control over is...YOUR OWN MIND. That is, if you learn how to exercise it.

Luckily, this one thing -- your mind -- that you do have control over gives you tremendous power. By exercising control over your mind, you can get the rest of those infinite other parts of the universe to begin to march in formation.

The person who says, "If I'm creating this, it certainly isn't on purpose," is right. They are not creating what is happening to them "on purpose." Who would purposely create failure, or bad relationships, or any other kind of suffering? You can only do something that is not good for you that is harmful to you, if you do it subconsciously. This means if you are creating something you don't want, you must be doing so subconsciously.

Your mind is running on automatic pilot, based on "software" (subconscious programming) installed when you were too young to know any better, by parents, teachers, friends, the media, and other experiences and influences. The key is to become more conscious, more aware...to get yourself off automatic pilot. Once you do this, you stop creating all the dramas and other garbage you don't want in your life.

How do you do this? One way is by remembering and using a very important piece of wisdom. What is this important piece of wisdom? I'm glad you asked.

It's the fact that whatever you focus on manifests as reality in your life.

You are always focusing on something, whether you are aware of it or not. If I spent some time with you, and heard your history, I could tell you what you are focusing on. How? By looking at the results you are getting in your life. The results you get are always the result of your focus.

The problem is this focus is usually not conscious focus; it's automatic or subconscious focus. We subconsciously focus on something we don't want, and then when we get it we feel like a victim and don't even stop to think that we created it in the first place. And what is more, we don't realize we could choose to create something completely different if we could only get out of the cycle of subconsciously focusing on something other than what we want.

If you have a significant negative emotional experience (say, for instance, a relationship in which you are abused or mistreated in some way), a part of you is going to say: "Okay, I get it. There are people out there who can and will hurt me. Relationships can be dangerous and painful.

I have to watch out for these people [or sometimes, relationships in general] and avoid them." Unfortunately, to watch out for them and avoid them, you have to focus your mind on "people who could hurt me," or "bad relationships," and that focus draws more of what you don't want to you...AND...actually makes these things you don't want (at least initially) attractive to you, so when they appear in your life you are drawn to them. This is why many people keep having one relationship after another with the same person, but in different bodies. This, of course, applies to everything, not just relationships. I'm just using relationships as an example.

Focusing on what you do not want, ironically, makes it happen. Focusing on not being poor makes you poor. Focusing on not making mistakes causes you to make mistakes. Focusing on not having a bad relationship creates bad relationships. Focusing on not being depressed makes you depressed. Focusing on not smoking makes you want to smoke. And so on. I think you get the idea. The mind will create what you focus on both GOOD and BAD!!!

The truth is your mind cannot tell the difference between something you think about or focus on that you DO want, and something you think about or focus on but do NOT want. The mind is a goal-seeking mechanism, and an extremely effective one at that. Already, all the time, it is elegantly and precisely creating exactly what you focus on. You are already a World Champion Expert at creating whatever you focus on. You couldn't get any better at it, and you don't need to get any better at it.

When you focus on anything, your mind says: "Okay, we can do that," and starts figuring out how to do it. It doesn't ask whether you're focusing on it because you want it or because you do not want it. It ALWAYS assumes you want what you focus on and then it goes and makes it happen. The more frequent and the more intense the focus, the faster and more completely you will create what you have focused on, which is why intense negative experiences create intense focus on what you do not want, and tend to make you re-create what you don't want, over and over.

Most of the time, for most people, all the focusing and thinking is going by at warp speed, on automatic, without much, if any, conscious intention. Your job is to learn how to direct this power by consciously directing your focus to the outcomes you want. Once you do, everything changes. This does, however, take some work, because at first you have to swim upstream against the current of your old, unconscious habits, and the current can be swift and strong. Trained observation actually teaches you to focus on what you want.

First, you have to discover all the things you focus on that you do not want, and I'm willing to bet there are quite a few -- way more than you think. To the degree you're getting what you don't want, you are focusing, albeit subconsciously, on what you don't want.

Spend some time over the next few weeks making a list of all the things you do NOT want as you notice yourself thinking about them.

Second, you have to get very clear about what you DO want. Then, you have to examine each of the things you want and be sure they are not just something you do NOT want in disguise. For instance, saying "I want a relationship where I am treated well" would not even be an issue if you had not had relationships where you were not treated well, and even in making this seemingly positive statement you are focusing on not wanting to be mistreated. Saying "I want a reliable car" wouldn't even come up if you weren't focusing on the fact that you don't want a car that breaks down and needs a lot of repairs.

After you've sorted out the things you habitually focus on that you do not want, and know what you do want, you have to begin to notice each time you think about an outcome you do not want, and consciously change your thinking, right in that moment, so you are instead focusing on what you do want.

Remember, you do NOT have to avoid things to be happy and get what you want. The urge to avoid something is a result of having had a negative emotional experience regarding that thing, and trying to avoid things requires you to focus on them, which tells your brain to create them. Not good.

You will be surprised how often you are thinking about what you do not want, how difficult it is to catch yourself doing it every time, and -- most of all – how difficult it is to switch your thinking to what you DO want. There is a strong momentum to keep thinking about that thing you want to avoid. As I said, the current is strong and swift, especially at first.

The solution? Practice, practice, practice. Persistence, persistence, persistence!!!

It's a very good idea to write down what you want, very specifically, so that your Fairy Godmother, were she to read it, would know exactly what to give you without any additional explanation.

28

Then, read what you have written to yourself, preferably out loud, several times a day, while seeing yourself, in your mind, already having what you want.

Believing is seeing and not the other way around as the world teaches you!

The more emotion you can bring to it, the better. Then, take whatever action is available to begin moving toward what you want. A good time to do this reading and visualizing is when you first wake up and before you go to bed.

I know this is work. Do it anyway. There is a price for everything, and this is the price you must pay to get what you want. Be prepared to pay it. It will be worth it, I promise. And be prepared to pay for a while before you get results. Stick with it.

Another way to change your focus is to ask questions. As an example, I'll ask you one right now. What did you have for breakfast this morning? To answer this question (even to just internally process the question), you had to shift your focus from whatever your mind was focused on (hopefully, to what I am teaching) to today's breakfast.

This means that to change your focus, all you have to do is...ask yourself a question!

It also means you better be careful what questions you ask yourself. Good questions include "How can I get X?" "How can I do X?" "How can I be X?" By asking these kinds of questions, you get your mind to focus on what you want to have, do, or be. Then, your mind takes over and answers the question...solves the problem...and creates what you want. You just have to provide the focus, take whatever action presents itself, and be persistent (some things take time).

I would do away with questions like "What's wrong with me?" or "Why can't I find someone to love me?" and so on. Your mind will find an answer to any question you give it, including these disempowering questions.

Learn to say "How can I...?" when you don't know what to do, instead of "I can't," and (if you are persistent in asking) you will receive the answer, every time. Learn to be conscious in what you focus on and your whole life will change.

This all may seem very utopian to you, or overly simplistic, or like a lot of work. I assure you it is not utopian (it's the way all successful people think), it IS simple, but not simplistic, and yes, it is work, at first. The great Napoleon Hill, who spent over 60 years studying the most effective and most successful people of the 20th century, concluded that -- without exception -- "whatever the mind can conceive and believe, it can achieve." He at first suspected there had to be exceptions, but toward the end of his life he said he had to admit he had not found ANY.

Let's go over that again: "Whatever the mind can conceive and believe it can achieve."

It will take some time to learn how to consciously focus your mind. It will require some effort. You will fail many times, and it will seem difficult. But at a certain point you will "get it" and at that point it will become as automatic as the unconscious focusing you have been doing. When that happens, a whole new universe of power will open to you.

More on Focusing

"And be not conformed to this age, but be transformed by the renewing of your mind, in order to prove by you what is the good and pleasing and perfect will of God."

The one thing in your life you can command is your own mind. Whatever negative people and situations you face, you can always choose a positive attitude. But doing so requires a firm, strong commitment.

Helpful: Begin by writing a self-convincing creed – I believe I can direct and control my emotions, intellect and habits with the intention of developing a positive mental attitude. Post it where you'll see it when you get up in the morning. Read it during the day, and say it aloud. Speaking an intention reinforces it. Choose a "self-motivator" – a meaningful phrase tailored to help you reach your positive thinking goals. Examples:

- Counter discouragement with the phrase "Every problem contains the seed of its own solution."

- Fight procrastination with "Do it now."

Keep your self-motivators nearby – in your pocket or on your desk – and repeat them throughout the day to instill these important new values.

Develop A Life Plan. Setting short and long-term goals each day creates a road map for your life. But only set GOOD goals!!! What is a good goal? One where you are 100% in control and one that is founded in love! A goal of raising good, healthy and prosperous children is a bad goal because you are not in control of what your kids choose. See the important difference? The goal is noble but it is not a good goal.

You identify where you're going, focus your mind on getting there and avoid many wrong turns.

Helpful: Use the D-E-S-I-R-E formula as a goal-setting guideline...

- **D**etermine what you want. Be exact, and express the goal positively. Say what you want to be or do rather than what you don't want.

- **E**valuate what you'll give in return. How much work will you do to turn your plan into action?

- **S**et a date for your goal. Be realistic, allowing enough time without postponing it too long.

- **I**dentify a step by step plan. Devise immediate, small steps to get started.

- **R**epeat your plan in writing.

- **E**ach and every day, morning and evening, read your plan aloud as you picture yourself already having achieved your goals.

Writing out your daily goals helps maintain your motivation. Keep them in your pocket or purse to read frequently throughout the day.

The Power of Visualization

Because visual images reach into our deepest mental levels, I have found pictures to be profound motivational tools. Why? Remember the mind holds everything as pictures!

Helpful: Make a list of personal qualities you want to develop…write down the names of people with whom you would like to have better relationships. Now clip pictures from magazines and newspapers that symbolize your goals.

Example: If generosity is your chosen quality, you could use a photo of someone with an outstretched hand.

Put the pictures where you'll see them everyday…and believe that you will get what you have visualized. You may also create your own "mental pictures" to defeat negative thoughts, such as dwelling on past reversals. Maintain A Positive Focus. Giving yourself positive experiences actually reinforces your positive attitude. Examples…

- Treat your five senses every day. Listen to your favorite music, taste a food you love, enjoy a beautiful view, etc.

- Cultivate a sense of humor. Laughter relaxes tension, and seeing the funny side of things helps you take yourself less seriously.

- Smile when you feel like frowning. Smile at yourself in the mirror. If this makes you laugh at yourself, the smile will be that much more real.

Now realize the optimistic face you show the world creates positive thoughts about you in everyone you meet.

How to Train Your Subconscious Mind

Did you know that often the difference between success and failure is the ability to train your mind to focus on achieving your goals and not focus on problems? It's been proven by researchers and by some of the most successful people in the world.

Getting your mind to focus and concentrate on success - so that it finds solutions instead of focusing on the problems is usually the difference between success and failure. But how do you do this?

I'm about to show you how. I'll outline the importance of training your mind, how to start directing your subconscious mind, and how to keep your mind focused so that you constantly achieve your goals and live the life you want. Disciplining your mind so that it is focused on your goals is crucial to your success. If your mind is not trained to focus on and achieve your goals then you really have little chance of success. Your conscious mind is a direct link to your subconscious mind.

So if your mind is focused on your goals and is trained to achieve those goals then your subconscious mind will also be focused on those goals and will attract the situations and opportunities for you to achieve the success you want. It's really that simple.

The minute you get distracted for a prolonged period - you lose sight of your objective and fail to accomplish those goals. In order for to enjoy success - the mind has to be regularly focused on your goals - you can't stay focused for short bursts and expect to get results.

Think of it this way, your riding in a car driven by your personal driver and every time your driver asks you where you want to go you simply say: "I don't know. Wherever you want to go is fine with me." Then when your driver takes you to the place of his choice you complain and say: "I don't want to be here, take me somewhere else." And again you say you don't know where you want to go.

Can you see the confusion you would create? Can you see how you would never get to where you want to go because you haven't traincd your driver to automatically take you where you want to go? You haven't given him the proper instructions.

Your mind and subconscious mind work the same way. If you don't train your mind to focus on your goals then your subconscious mind cannot create the situations that will help you achieve those goals. When you keep changing your mind, when you are not clear on what you want - your subconscious gets confused - and you end up exactly where you don't want to be.

Let's go back to the example of your personal driver. Wouldn't it be a lot easier and more comfortable if you told your driver where you wanted to go - or even better - your driver knew where you wanted to go ahead of time? But that will only happen when you train your driver by repeatedly telling him where you want to go on a regular basis.

Your subconscious mind is your driver. Your subconscious gets its instructions from your thoughts and beliefs. Give your subconscious the right instructions and it will take you where ever you want to go in life. When your mind is focused on your goals you direct your subconscious to create opportunities for you to achieve your goals. Your responsibility is to follow up on these opportunities.

How You Can Train Your Mind

Believe it or not I get a lot of calls and emails everyday from people who want to achieve their goals but simply can't get their mind to focus on the tasks that need to be done to have the success that they want. This happens because the mind is simply not used to focusing on your goals and following up with completing those tasks. So how do you get your mind to change? How do you train your mind?

The first step is to get the mind to stop doing what it is used to doing - or break the pattern that you've been following for so long. This will require some effort - but the reward will allow you to live the life you want and enjoy the level of success that you want.

To re-train your mind and direct your subconscious mind you start by paying more attention - so that when you see yourself getting distracted and not following up on things that you wanted to do - you take a step to break the pattern. You can break the pattern by doing something else. For example: you can start following up on what you had planned to do, you can create a list and follow up with it regularly to see if you are on track.

One thing that always works is to think about your goals every morning. As you're in bed, think about your goals and think about what you can do to achieve them during the day. If you find that you constantly say: "I don't know what do to do to achieve my goals." Then you're not looking for answers in the right place.

Take a look at what other people have done to achieve similar goals and see if you can follow the same process. For example: If you want to make more money take a

36

look at someone else who has made a lot of money and see what they've done. Can you follow their process? Maybe you can even talk to them about the process? If you want to meet someone and be in a healthy relationship, talk to a friend who is in a successful relationship and find out what they did. By doing the above exercises you train your mind to focus on finding solutions while at the same time you direct your subconscious mind to create the opportunities for you to succeed. And - you begin to create a new pattern of thinking and you start to train the mind to work differently. You're now telling your driver where you want to go. This eliminates the confusion and allows you to achieve your goals.

You're not going to magically get your mind to focus or concentrate without you taking some form of action. When you finally do take some action your mind will still resist - but as you continue taking action the resistance will subside - REPITITION. So what action can you take? First start with the exercise I just outlined above. Next - meditate. Meditation is one of the best ways to relax and calm your mind while training it to focus on what you want. When you meditate you actually start to clear the clutter that dominates your mind.

Make the Time

Finally it seems a lot of people have come to believe that they just don't have the time to achieve their goals. If you are one of the many who have such a belief then you've really convinced yourself that your goals are not worthy of your time; because if they were you would make the time for them. I'm not talking about spending an entire day or even a few hours. It's only a few minutes at different intervals. Why try to get everything crammed into one hour? Why not try to think about your goals at different intervals during the day? For example: you may have a few minutes while you're taking a walk - think of your achieving your goals. You could also do this while you're taking a shower, driving, walking, anytime. Here's a suggestion; the next time you are driving or taking a shower, pay attention to your thoughts. Are these thoughts actually working for your or against you? Would it be better to focus on your goals or keep recycling the negative clutter or junk in your head? The choice is yours - and taking action is really about taking a small step. You don't need to spend hours meditating. Even if you simply mediated for 5 or 10 minutes a day you'd be able to increase your ability to concentrate and focus by a 100-percent within a matter of days! Do it for weeks or months and you'll have dramatic results!

How to Put Your Mind to Sleep Quickly and Rest Completely

If you often lay awake, unable to put your mind to rest while you're tossing and turning, you're going to love what you're about to read, because I'm about to share with you one of the most powerful methods for quickly shutting off your mind, and drifting off to sleep.

As you may already know, your mind must be in the Alpha brain-wave stage to fall asleep. This is the stage your mind enters you're still conscious, but your body and begin to relax. It enables your more rampant and conscious mind to turn off as you enter the realm of sleep. We all know how it feels... when you're lying awake in bed trying to fall asleep, it seems like your mind is running on hyper-speed. It's almost like you're thinking

10 times faster than when you're just normally awake and alert. In fact, if you experience this often, I can tell you for a fact that your mind IS working harder than it is when you're not trying to fall asleep, and there is a very good reason for it, here's why this happens. In my books and articles on sleep, I often teach a principle: "What you focus on expands." You see, your mind responds to focus, and it goes hand in hand with the law of momentum. What is the law of momentum? Quite simply:

"Energy in motion, tends to STAY in motion"

"Energy stopped, tends to STAY stopped"

In other words, if you take action in your life, and begin to create success, you will experience more and more success every day. Success breeds success. On the other hand, if you sit your butt down on the couch to watch TV and say, "Aww, just one show, I'll only watch one show," very soon you'll be sitting there for four hours, and you'll watch five or six shows.

The law of momentum is everywhere in life, in physics, with your body, and most importantly, with your "thoughts." You see, your thinking is very predictable; it all works on the law of focus and momentum. Your mind is like a big ball of potential thinking energy, just waiting for you to give it a direction to think wildly into. It awaits and responds your every command. It's an exceptional tool except, most of us aren't very experienced at "controlling" this amazing tool. In fact, a lot people aren't even aware that they can control it! And this is where sleep problems come in.

Imagine your mind like a giant overflowing lake that's just waiting for an outlet to pour into... Slowly, when it finds an outlet, it begins with a trickle of water. That trickle turns into a stream. Then, that stream turns into a small river. Pretty soon, the small river is a giant unstoppable waterfall. Your thoughts work in the same way when you're "trying" to fall asleep.

For example, you're lying in bed, frustrated, forcing your mind to not think. "I just want to get some sleep! Stop thinking! Okay, starting now... I won't think anymore. No think... nothing. My life is nothing... If only I would finally get motivated in my job maybe I would finally create the income to start traveling instead of dealing with these problems. Problems, how can I... Ahh, I'm thinking again! Stop it!"

You get even more frustrated, and repeat the process over again in a few minutes. So how do you stop it? It's easy, you see, you can easily control your thinking, except most people aren't aware of the tools necessary! The good news is, I'm about to give you the 3-step handbook to controlling your mind. Here are the 3-universal steps that will enable you to not only stop thinking; you'll also be able to lower your brain-waves into the alpha brain-state, which will quickly let you enter sleep...

Awareness

The first step to changing anything is becoming aware that it's happening, especially if it's your mind. Pretend your mind is racing, and you finally realize that you're thinking... Most people at this stage get extremely frustrated and "try" to force the mind into submission. It doesn't work! Why? Because, what you focus on

40

expands. The more frustrated you get, the more you're focusing on frustration, so you'll get even MORE frustration and more thinking... on and on!

So the first step is to simply become "aware" of the fact that you're thinking. Nothing more. When you notice that you're thinking, smile to yourself, and say, "I just noticed myself thinking... Interesting..." Now notice what happens inside of you when you do this... something VERY profound. If "I" just noticed "myself" thinking, perhaps there are really two completely separate identities running your life? There is the "I" and there is the "self."

The "I", is the real you, the higher being, the "I" behind the mind, that runs the show, the heart, the soul, the true conscious being, the choice maker.

The "self" is the mind; if left to run the show, it will run in endless circles until the edge of insanity.

The moment you do this, the moment you become "aware" - you are no longer a slave to your mind. You have won. After you become aware... do nothing, just lay there for 3 seconds and notice how it feels to be present in who you really are, not the mind, but you, the "I" - there is a great feeling of peace behind that presence in the "I." Why? Because when you are aware like this, you're aware of the power of your choice making. You now have the power of choice.

Relaxed Focus

"What you focus on expands." Now that you have become aware of your thinking, all you have to do is "direct" your mind into a place that will bring you into a deep, deep place of relaxation. Think about it, if before

41

your mind will relentlessly race into any direction you give it; why not pick a direction that will give you peace and restful sleep?

But, most people don't know what that direction really is. It's really easy. If you focus on anything your body does or feels subconsciously, you will begin to become more and more realized. For example your breathing, the feeling of the pillow on your head, the sounds of nature outside (unless you live in the city), the warmth of your body. These are all things that happen, yet your conscious mind doesn't think about them.

As you know, "What you focus on expands"... So what would happen if you focused on something that is happening in your "subconscious"? That's right, your conscious thinking would diminish, and your subconscious mind would begin to take over the entire process of you falling asleep! It really is that simple, and it works every-time.

The easiest one is your breathing. And I promise you if you just try this tonight, you will be shocked when you wake up in the morning: "Wow! It worked!"

Repetition

As I said, the easiest one to focus on is your breathing. In the beginning, you'll find this easier said than done. Let me walk you through it.

- Begin by taking your focus onto your breathing. Take a deep breath in. Hold it for a short while, and slowly exhale...
- Count "1"

- Breathe in again... hold it shortly, exhale slowly, and count...

- "2"

Why count? Because I guarantee you, in the very beginning, you may find it challenging to hold your focus. In fact, you'll be surprised as you may not even make it to "5" the first time. This is because your conscious ever-thinking mind will butt in and interrupt. You may randomly go off into a barrage of thoughts again. If this happens, and it very well may, what do you do?

Simply become aware, and begin focusing on your breathing again. Guess what happens? As you become aware, 2 or 3 times... your mind will give up. I guarantee you, beyond the shadow of a doubt, when you get to "10" or "15" breaths you will feel a wave of relaxation in your body. This is the silent "click" as your mind shifts from the high frequency Beta brain-waves into Alpha brain-waves. Your subconscious mind will do the rest!

The following exercise will teach you how to see and recognize things that are unworthy of attention, but still recognize that they are there. In other words, attention will be paid to it and then discarded. A filter makes you totally oblivious (no attention given to it at all) that the stimuli are there and if asked to describe the situation, the filter will cause you to omit it.

Chapter 2 – What Is In It For You to Lie, Cheat & Deceive

Me, I'm dishonest, and you can always trust a dishonest man to be dishonest. Honestly, it's the honest ones you have to watch out for.
Johnny Depp

Where is the gain for people who lie, cheat and deceive? This is an important question to ask too.

In Chapter 1, I explained the difference between true reality that the conscious mind SEES and the PERCEIVED reality that the subconscious mind uses. There is a difference and the difference is quite large.

A liar, cheater and deceiver does perceive a big gain in their behavior, otherwise they would not do what they do. This perception is a wrongful belief system and hence; their gain is a false gain.

But candidly, even a false gain is worthy of their actions even if this appears silly on the surface. In essence the very first person they deceive is themselves.

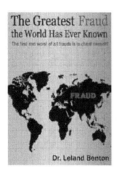

In my book, "The Greatest Fraud The World Has Ever Known," In my book, I go to the root of the problem of self deception.

http://www.amazon.com/dp/B008GUBKI2

"The Greatest Fraud The World Has Ever Known" is the person practicing deception because they are only fooling themselves into believing that this is a lifestyle worth pursuing.

Here is an excerpt from my book...

In today's world, fraud is running rampant. But in actuality, fraud is not new concept. From the beginning of time man has used deception from everything such as war to love.

In the animal kingdom, animals use deception for protection by the use of camouflage and more.

45

The high technology of our times makes access to all forms of information almost instantaneous and the news media sensationalizes fraud to a point of frenzy.

Fraud is defined as intentional deception made for personal gain or to damage another individual.

In recent years, top fraudsters such as Bernie Madoff, Ken Lay and Jeff Skilling of Enron, Allen Stanford, Bernie Ebbers of Worldcom, Dennis Kozlowski of Tyco International, Martin Frankel, James Lewis, Lou Pearlman of N'Sync fame, Barry Minkow of ZZZZ Best, and Tom Petters have been brought to justice and given lengthy prison terms.

No one seemingly escapes fraud; everyone on the planet has been deceived in some manner.

As Chief Forensics Investigator for ForensicsNation.com, I compile and preserve evidence of cyber-crime fraud all the time.

Cyber crime is rampant too and growing; you would not believe how exposed the average citizen is today.

Society has come to rely on computers, cell phones, and computer-run public systems such as traffic lights, food distribution, water supply and much more in such a way that any disruption of these services jeopardizes our quality of life.

People make use of Wi-Fi systems inside their homes, in public places such as libraries and Starbucks, which make them huge targets for hackers and crackers.

As a behavioral scientist, I have studied the criminal mind and have made many conclusions.

Recently we busted a voyeur using a wireless camera to spy on a Hooters waitress while she was undressing in her apartment. We caught him a couple of blocks away in his car with a handheld viewing device.

When I played back what he had seen for the waitress, her comment was, "Why? He could see more on the Internet."

And yes, it is true, you can Google just about any body part you want and see more on the Internet but the waitress missed the one important factor that causes crime - the thrill of getting away with something that is forbidden!

When a person thinks of fraud, rarely do they ever think along the lines of defrauding themselves but yet this is the most common occurrences of fraud.

Self deception runs rampant in our respective psyches; the ability to deceive ourselves cannot be minimized.

This book addresses this self deception and our inherent need to defraud ourselves.

We defraud ourselves in many ways; too many to list here but here is a partial list: the way we eat, how much we eat, our diets in general, our looks, our need to be loved, sex, our need to achieve, our beliefs, and more.

The total essences of our lives are completely affected by self deception; most of our personal existences cannot be lived without the deceptions we have created.

Let me give you an example: A person buys an automobile that they really cannot afford because it provides a status symbol of success. In many people's minds, a high-priced automobile means they "made it" but the reality is they haven't made it at all unless you count making themselves a slave to the monthly bill that pays for the automobile.

The reality of the high monthly payment takes a back seat to the perception of the automobile being a status symbol.

People overeat to assuage some pain due to stress and anxiety. They deceive themselves into believing that eating takes their minds off their problems.

They lie, gossip and deceive because it brings others that they perceive are above them down to their level.

This is the main cause of bullying and malicious gossip. We all do it; maybe not to a point where something really bad occurs like suicide, but we all still do it.

Without a doubt, we deceive ourselves the most when it comes to looks and beauty. Everything from anorexia to tanning to the clothes we wear top the list of self deception due to concerns over how a person looks.

Why are physical things leading the list of self deceptions? Why aren't the mental things at the top? After all, all of our self deceptions originate in the subconscious mind.

In this book, I will attempt to answer these questions and more. I will examine our need for self deception and the results of practicing this interesting human trait.

I will offer examples for you to ponder and that will demonstrate the core essential of my premises. None of what I present must be taken as a given; deception is subjective, which means it becomes anything you want it to become.

What is objective here is studying my core essential premises and weighing them against your own existence. A thorough and object examination of yourself may become painful but you will quickly realize that your own self deceptions rob you of a quiet and peaceful existence.

One objective fact is quite persistent throughout this book - The Greatest Fraud the World Has Ever Known is YOU!

Self-Deception is rampant and it isn't going to go away as long as the person practicing it perceives it as something of value.

It is quite easy to deceive yourself and a person can rationalize this deception in so many ways that it literally boggles the mind. Even with the facts known and presented to the person, the urge and need to keep the deception going is huge.

Let me give you an example…

Recently on Amazon.com I was personally attacked in the Amazon forum by a "gang" of people that had appointed themselves as Amazon Review Cops. They were harassing authors claiming that their reviews of their books were faked and they were paid reviews. They went on to accuse me as being a "paid reviewer" because I write a good many reviews.

No amount of reasoning appeased these people so I reported them to Amazon along with a plethora of authors that they had also attacked. I then filed criminal stalking charges and a federal district lawsuit for damages.

You should have heard the howl and the cry from this gang of people. They wrote to Amazon to complain that I had targeted them and were being unfair filing criminal charges and a civil lawsuit.

Amazon's response was to tell them not to harass authors with unfounded accusations or in other words…tough, you are on your own.

Now, this gang perceived they were doing good when all they were doing was putting on a false front for what they really wanted to do, which was harass authors. They cared nothing about the reviews; they only wanted the authors to engage them in the forum where this gang could literally "tear them apart' and ruin their brand and reputation.

What they didn't expect was ME! This "homey" don't play no games and this gang never even considered the consequences of an author fighting back. It was so shocking to them that the majority of the gang wrote to me apologizing for their actions and asking to be removed from the suit. My response: "NO WAY!" Each gang member is accountable for their actions and they will pay the price for ruining brands and reputations. BTW – I had given them fair warning that if they continued in their behavior that I would file a criminal complaint and civil lawsuit; they just didn't believe it.

Here is my point and it is a big one: a person IS ALWAYS accountable for their actions and even if you deceive yourself into believing that your actions are justified then be prepared to defend yourself in a court of law. You are not invisible on the Internet.

Now let's move on to why people lie…

Chapter 3 – Why People Lie

I get no respect. The way my luck is running, if I was a politician I would be honest.
Rodney Dangerfield

The answer to why people lie is varied so bear with me if I become overly verbose in my answer.

The first reason is called "scarcity thought" and I have discussed this in detail in the "Why" series of books.

Scarcity thought is basically where a person perceives that everybody is getting their share of good and they are being left out. The keyword here is "perceived".

Scarcity thought is a very prevalent "belief system" and a good many people truly perceive that they are being left out of their good.

The second most common reason is fantasy. In my book, "Fantasy Is easy – Everything Is Perfect," I describe the problems of a fantasy life that is out of control.

http://www.amazon.com/dp/B00BFF81CS

This reason is more prevalent than scarcity thought actually since everyone on the planet engages is some sort of fantasy life. And a fantasy life is not bad unless it manifests itself in reality and the person begins to believe that their fantasy is truly reality.

I give an example of a person at a party telling people that he is the King of France. Everyone knows he is lying and they whisper behind his back that he is crazy. Now this person knows that everyone at this party knows he is lying but he doesn't care…why? Because he is not in their world; he is in his world and in his world he is a King! Get it?

He is not in their world of reality; he is in his world of fantasy and as he walks up and down in his world he could care less what people are saying. They aren't a part of his world. This is how damaging a fantasy life can be if left unchecked.

Unfortunately, fantasy truly is easy and truly everything is perfect in a fantasy. It doesn't cost anything to create a fantasy life but the cost is real when it manifests itself in crazy and weird behavior.

Here is an excerpt from my book, "Fantasy Is easy – Everything Is Perfect,"

It is a known fact within the research confines of behavioral science that the human subconscious mind cannot tell the difference between fantasy and reality. For example: your conscious mind knows that you are sitting in a movie theater watching a movie but your subconscious mind does not and when a sad scene comers along, you respond with the same emotions as if the scene was real...maybe you cry, get angry, or simply melancholy.

In this book, I will begin in Chapter 1 with "Laying a Proper Foundation" that deals with the mechanism of the human mind and how the mind functions both conscious mind and subconscious mind.

There has been as good many news stories recently dealing with people that have committed horrible crimes – Sandy Hook Elementary School, Aurora, CO Movie Theater killings, etc – and the questions usually raised first deal with violent video games, and the things that may have influenced behavior or cause these acts of violence.

You may see yourself within these pages. The adventure I am about to take you on may be painful but I promise, you will become a better person because of your participation.

"Former Arizona congresswoman Gabrielle Giffords looked in the eyes of the man who shot her today and, through her husband, said she is now "done thinking about you." Giffords was sitting in the second row of the courtroom with her husband, ex-astronaut Mark Kelly

and she stretched to get a better view of Jared Loughner when he entered the courtroom. http://abcnews.go.com/US/gabrielle-giffords-tells-shooter-shes-thinking/story?id=17672546

Unfortunately, when acts of violence occur, the media takes the opportunity to assign causes and reasons that simply are not founded in science and are untrue.

The same can be said of James Eagan Holmes the killer behind the Aurora, Colorado movie theater violence. On Friday, July 20, 2012, a mass shooting occurred inside of a Century movie theater in Aurora, Colorado, during a midnight screening of the film The Dark Knight Rises. A gunman, dressed in tactical clothing, set off tear gas grenades and shot into the audience with multiple firearms, killing 12 people and injuring 58 others. The sole suspect is James Eagan Holmes, who was arrested outside the cinema minutes later.

The media blamed it on Loughner's penchant for violent video games, when in fact; he is suffering from a plethora of mental diseases.

Furthermore, on December 14, 2012, 20-year-old Adam Lanza fatally shot twenty children and six adult staff members at Sandy Hook Elementary School in the village of Sandy Hook in Newtown, Connecticut. Before driving to the school, Lanza had shot and killed his mother, Nancy, at their Newtown home. As first responders arrived, he committed suicide by shooting himself in the head. The incident was the second deadliest school shooting in United States history, after the 2007 Virginia

55

Tech massacre. It was also the second-deadliest mass murder at an American elementary school, after the 1927 Bath School bombings in Michigan. The shooting prompted renewed debate about gun control in the United States, and a proposal for new legislation banning the sale and manufacture of certain types of semi-automatic weapons and magazines with more than ten rounds of ammunition.

The media and government always use these acts of violence for sound bites and to push hidden agendas when in actuality the causes and reasons may be obscured or not readily apparent.

This is sad because most often the real reasons behind these acts of violence go unanswered to the general public and they are left with wrong impressions and a sense of confusion and hopelessness.

The debate is not whether guns, ammunition and magazines are necessary or should be limited. The debate and conversation should center on the causes of such acts of violence and what can be done to limit whatever it is that triggers such violence.

In my experience, just about anything you want is available for the right price. Even if guns were completely outlawed, criminal types and obviously mentally unbalanced people would still find a way to obtain them.

It is important to note that every situation is different. Each perpetrator of crimes of violence cannot be labeled or shoved into a particular "slot" of reason or circumstance.

It is easy to blame mental disease for a plethora of manifested behaviors and in many cases this would be true but not always. It makes a good defense in court but many cases claiming mental incompetence are being shot down by psychologist as being shams.

I want to now examine other causes of manifested behavior stemming from living a life within a fantasy.

I made a list and I will expand on this list as we go along...

- *Childhood Causes – these are causes that develop within the course of a person's upbringing. It takes into account many of the factors listed below including childhood trauma, maturity, and environment. How we are raised, where we are raised and what type of an environment we are raised in all play a factor in a person's eventual adult existence.*

- *Childhood Trauma – a good many children suffer from many types of childhood traumas including physical and verbal abuse, molestation, bullying, disease, and more. These traumas can manifest themselves immediately or later on in adult life.*

- *Child Rearing – the way we are raised bears a good deal on how and what we become in our adult lives. Economic conditions have forced*

57

both parents into the workplace and children are left to themselves or day care facilities. The home environment contributes heavily to the problem especially if parents often fight because of finances, poor marital relations or whatever causes a tenuous home environment.

- **Maturity** – this is probably one of the most contributing factors to embracing a fantasy life since a person's maturity level bears a direct influence on how a person handles all situations in life. Remember, it is easy to be drawn into a fantasy life because everything in a fantasy life is perfect and free.

- **Mimicking Behavior Patterns** - A child that grows up in a home of violence tends to be violent. Parents that smoke and drink tend to raise children that exhibit the same behavior. Children will observe and mimic all types of behavior that they see their parents do as well as other adults and children. If left unchecked, these behavioral patterns can become set for life.

- **Environment** – the environment in which we are raised and live is the second most important factor contributing to the withdrawal into a fantasy life. It is easy to retreat into a world that the person deems as perfect. We tend to dream of the perfect but live in the flawed!! If we cannot change our physical environment then we can withdraw into a world that is far more satisfying than the one we actually live in.

- **Self-Entertainment** – *this is a contributing factor that cannot be dismissed since I see it occurring almost daily. In the past, we called it daydreaming and it was deemed seemingly innocuous. Today, we now know that this trait is practiced by individuals far more often than first believed. It has become the scourge of the workplace as individuals withdraw into their own worlds leaving workloads untouched. Young people complain that the opposite gender only wants entertainment and fun with no commitment. Many complain that the opposite gender is in a world unto themselves and in many cases this is true.*

- **Pathological Liars** – *this is not a matter of low self-esteem; in fact it usually is a case of too much self-esteem. And more and more cases are being recorded where the individual lies but is not considered a pathological liar. Everybody lies; this is a given, but the reasons behind the lie determine the extent of which a person will go to keep his fantasy life going. In this case, the fantasy life is most important. Let me give you an example: I am going to tell you a lie right now. Ready? I am the King of France! Now you know this is a lie; France no longer has a monarchy. And I know that you know I am lying but I don't care because I am not in your world of reality; I am in my fantasy world and in my world I rule as king.*

It is important to note that the factors cited above can also contribute to a very satisfying and mentally sound adult life too. The door swings both ways.

*****

The causes of fantasy are actually the same causes of lies, cheats and deception in a more varied format. Go back and read them carefully; they describe some very disturbed individuals suffering from many different kinds of disorder and these people you have contact with daily.

Thankfully most of them are harmless but it only takes one to snap and cause the carnage described above.

Now let's discuss why people cheat and philander…

Chapter 4 – Why People Cheat

Ninety eight percent of the adults in this country are decent, hardworking, honest Americans. It's the other lousy two percent that get all the publicity. But then, we elected them.
Lily Tomlin

Cheating on a spouse or girlfriend is as old as the hills themselves but cheating in general takes on many forms such as cheating on an exam, cheating on your taxes, and cheating on your driver's license test, etc.

Why people cheat has a many varied response just like in Chapter 3 and you may even see yourself in my words. But don't worry; I won't leave you hanging. In Chapter 6, I will show you how to correct this.

Cheating is more than a character flaw; cheating is the result of a lustful lifestyle and I am not speaking in strictly sexual terms here.

Lust is counterfeit love. Where love grows; lust needs to be renewed and this "renewal' takes the form of cheating.

It is easy to see how lust and sex are combined; a wandering mate may have grown tired of the sex and is looking for a bigger thrill. But lust and cheating in various other scenarios may take a minute to grasp.

Cheating means that a person is willing to use alternative means to gain something they feel they cannot achieve or is unwilling to make the effort to achieve it.

A cheater is not only immoral; they are lazy too. Here is an article from Wikipedia that gives examples of cheating; some of which you have never imagined...

Cheating
From Wikipedia, the free encyclopedia

http://en.wikipedia.org/wiki/Cheating

Cheating *refers to an immoral way of achieving a goal. It is generally used for the breaking of rules to gain advantage in a competitive situation. Cheating is the getting of reward for ability by dishonest means. This broad definition will necessarily include acts of bribery, cronyism, sleaze, nepotism and any situation where individuals are given preference using inappropriate criteria. The rules infringed may be explicit, or they may be from an unwritten code of conduct based on morality, ethics or custom, making the identification of cheating a subjective process. Cheating can refer specifically to marital infidelity. Someone who is known for cheating is* referred to as a cheat in British English, and a cheater in American English. A "cheat" does not have to cheat all the time, but once faced with a challenge that they do actually want to win, they will go back to their cheating strategies.

Sport, games and gambling

Sports are governed by both customs and explicit rules regarding acts which are permitted and forbidden at the event and away from it. Forbidden acts frequently include performance-enhancing drug taking (known as "doping"), using equipment that does not conform to the rules or altering the condition of equipment during play, and deliberate harassment or injury to competitors.

High profile examples of alleged cheating include Lance Armstrong, Ben Johnson's disqualification following the 100 metres final at the 1988 Summer Olympics, and admissions of steroid use by former professional baseball players after they have retired, such as José Canseco and Ken Caminiti.

One of the most famous instances of cheating occurred during the 1986 FIFA World Cup quarter-final, when Diego Maradona used his hand to punch the ball into the goal of England goalkeeper Peter Shilton. Another example of this, more recently was Luis Suarez's handball during the quarter finals of the 2010 FIFA World Cup when in the dying seconds he punched the ball off the line, preventing a clear Ghana goal. Using the hand or arm by anyone other than a goalkeeper is illegal according to the rules of association football.

Illegally altering the condition of playing equipment is frequently seen in sports such as baseball and cricket. For example in baseball, a pitcher using a doctored baseball (e.g. putting graphite or Vaseline on the baseball), or a batter using a corked bat are some examples of this.

Circumvention of rules governing conduct and procedures of a sport can also be considered cheating. During the 2007 Formula One Season, driver Fernando Alonso was labeled a "cheat" for exchanging confidential information between the teams of Scuderia Ferrari and Mclaren.

Gambling

The wagering of money on an event extends the motivation for cheating beyond directly participating competitors. As in sport and games, cheating in gambling is generally related to directly breaking rules or laws, or misrepresenting the event being wagered on, or interfering in the outcome. A boxer who takes a dive, a casino which plays with secretly loaded dice, a rigged roulette wheel or slot machine, or a doctored deck of cards, are generally regarded as cheating, because it has misrepresented the likelihood of the game's outcomes beyond what is reasonable to expect a bettor to protect himself against. However, for a bookmaker to flatter a horse in order to sell bets on it at shorter odds may be regarded as salesmanship rather than cheating, since bettors can counter this by informing themselves and by exercising skepticism. Doping a horse is a clear example of cheating by interfering with the instruments of the event under wager. Again, not all interference is cheating; spending money to support the health and well-being of a horse one has wagered on is not in itself generally regarded as cheating, nor is improving the morale of a sportsman one has backed by cheering for them. Generally, interference is more likely to be regarded as cheating if it diminishes the standard of a sporting competition, damages a participant, or modifies the apparatus of the event or game.

In the world of gambling, knowing a secret which is not priced into the odds gives a significant advantage, which may give rise to a perception of cheating. However, legal systems do not regard secretly making use of knowledge in this way as criminal deception in itself. This is in contrast to the financial world, where people with certain categories of relationship to a company are restricted from transacting, which would constitute the crime of insider trading. This may be because of a stronger presumption of equality between investors, or it may be because a company employee who also trades in the company's stock has a conflict of interest, and has thus misrepresented himself the company. An advantage player typically uses mental, observational or technical skills to choose when and how much to bet and neither interferes with the instruments of the game nor breaks any of its rules. Representatives of the casino industry have claimed that all advantage play is cheating, but this point of view is reflected neither among societies in general nor in legislation. As of 2010, the only example anywhere of a type of advantage play being unlawful is for an advantage player to use an auxiliary device in the U.S. State of Nevada, whose legislation is uniquely influenced by large casino corporations. Nonetheless it remains a widely held principle that the law should not impose any restraint over the method by which a player arrives at a playing or betting decision from information held by him lawfully and which he is not debarred from under the rules of the game. In "hole carding", however, a casino player tries to catch sight of the front of cards which are dealt face-down according to the rules. Hole carding is more susceptible to the charge of cheating, since the rules may explicitly forbid the player from knowing the card in question. One way of cheating and profiting through gambling is to bet against yourself and then intentionally lose. This is known as throwing a game or taking a dive. Illegal gamblers will at times pay sports players to lose so that they may profit from the otherwise unexpected loss. An especially notorious case is the Black Sox Scandal, when eight players of the 1919 Chicago White Sox took payment from gamblers and intentionally played poorly.

Strength training

Cheating is also used to refer to movements in strength training that transfer weight from an isolated or fatigued muscle group to a different or fresh muscle group. This allows the cheater to move an initial greater weight (if the cheating continues through an entire training set) or to continue exercising past the point of muscular exhaustion (if the cheating begins part way through the set). As strength training is not a sport, cheating has no rule-based consequences, but can result in injury or a failure to meet training goals. This is because each exercise is designed to target specific muscle groups and if the proper form is not used the weight can be transferred away from the targeted group.

Personal relationships

In western and other cultures, couples usually expect sexual monogamy of each other. If so, then cheating commonly refers to forms of infidelity, particularly adultery. However, there are other divisions of infidelity, which may be emotional. Cheating by thinking of, touching and talking with someone may be equally damaging to one of the parties. Not only physical infidelity is considered cheating. Cheating on your partner could also include something like chatting online with somebody. Online infidelity is also a way to cheat on a significant other. Emotional cheating may be a form of emotional abuse, which to date is treated seriously in a court of law as physical cheating. With the expansion of understanding of other cultures, there is a wide spectrum of what cheating means. When in a committed relationship, the definition of cheating is based on both parties' opinions, and both parties may redefine their understanding to match the party at an either lower or higher extreme of this definition. Cheating constitutes doing anything, whether verbal or physical, that one would not do in front of their significant other. Such examples would include: expressing attraction to another person, talking, electronic communications, texting, data, cybering, and sexual contact.

Many people consider cheating to be any violation of the mutually agreed-upon rules or boundaries of a relationship, which may or may not include sexual monogamy. For example, in some polygamous relationships, the concepts of commitment and fidelity do not necessarily hinge on complete sexual or emotional monogamy. Whether polygamous or monogamous, the boundaries to which people agree vary widely, and sometimes these boundaries evolve within each relationship.

In video games

In video games, cheating can take the form of secret access codes in single-player games (such as the Konami code) which unlock a bonus for the player when entered, and add-ons or exploits which give players an unfair advantage in online multiplayer games.

Attitudes towards cheating vary. On one hand, cheating allows casual players to complete games at much-accelerated speed, which can be helpful in some cinematic or one-player games, which can take a subjectively long time to finish, as is typical of the Role-Playing Game (RPG) genre. While this may be seen as a hasty advantage, and causing no damage to anyone, in a multi-player game such as MMORPGs the repercussions of cheating are much more damaging. Cheating in those types of games is often prohibited. In many circles, the purchasing of items or currency from sources outside the game is also considered to be cheating. The Terms of Service from many games where this is possible directly prohibits this activity. An example would be, in the Pokémon franchise the player can hack for items and Pokémon unavailable at that time or in that game, and they can hack for experience gain to level their party to become incredibly powerful early.

In First Person Shooter (FPS) games, players can use multihacks containing different kind of cheats. These include: Aimbot (automatically aims at targets), Wallhack (allows the cheater to see targets through walls), and ESP (displays information about the targets).

Another form of video game cheating is when a player does things unforeseen by the programmers to permit changes to the way enemies are encountered (or objectives met). This could be through means of a "Hack" where altered game files are substituted for the normal files, or image graphics changed to permit greater visibility of the targets, etc.

Another type of cheat would be an exploit cheat where an advantage is gained through an unintended game exploit, such as skipping a weapon reload timer by quickly switching weapons back and forth without actually reloading the weapons. Generally speaking, there is often some concern that this is not truly cheating, as it is the fault of the programmers that such an exploit exists in the first place. However, technically, as with live sports, it is cheating if the player is not playing the game in a formally approved manner, breaking unwritten rules. In some cases, this behavior is directly prohibited by the Terms of Service of the game.

Academic

There is enough evidence to conclude that academic cheating is an extremely common occurrence in high schools and colleges in the United States. 70% of public high school students admit to serious test cheating. 60% say they have plagiarized papers. Only 50% of private school students, however, admit to this. The report was made in June 2005 by Rutgers University professor Donald McCabe for The Center for Academic Integrity. The findings were corroborated in part by a Gallup survey. In McCabe's 2001 of 4500 high school students, "74% said they cheated on a test, 72% cheated on a written work, and 97% reported to at least had copied someone's homework or peeked at someone's test. 1/3 reported to have repeatedly cheated." The new revolution in high-tech digital info contributes enormously to the new wave in cheating: online term-paper mills sell formatted reports on practically any topic; services exist to prepare any kind of homework or take online tests for students, despite the fact that this phenomenon, and these websites, are well known to educators, and camera phones are used to send pictures of tests; MP3 players can hold digitalized notes; graphing calculators store formulas to solve math problems. Increased competition for college admissions in recent years may also be to blame. It is often justified by "Homework help", "group work" or "little more practice".

*****

As you can see, cheating comes in a variety of scenarios and many are very creative. What is your definition of cheating? Some classify cheating in different categories from "little white lies" being okay to downright fibbing being un-okay.

Here is the dictionary definition of cheating:

cheat   ē

No matter how you define it, cheating is wrong! And cheating is a form of deception.

Now let's talk about deception...

Chapter 5 – Why People Deceive

There's one way to find out if a man is honest - ask him. If he says, "Yes," you know he is a crook.
Groucho Marx

Deception is the parent of all lies and cheating. As in lies and cheating in general, deception takes on many forms and in many cases is justified as described in the following article:

Deception
From Wikipedia, the free encyclopedia

http://en.wikipedia.org/wiki/Deception

Deception, beguilement, deceit, bluff, mystification and **subterfuge** *are acts to propagate beliefs that are not true, or not the whole truth (as in half-truths or omission).*

Deception can involve dissimulation, propaganda, and sleight of hand, as well as distraction, camouflage, or concealment. There is also self-deception, as in bad faith.

Deception is a major relational transgression that often leads to feelings of betrayal and distrust between relational partners. Deception violates relational rules and is considered to be a negative violation of expectations. Most people expect friends, relational partners, and even strangers to be truthful most of the time. If people expected most conversations to be untruthful, talking and communicating with others would require distraction and misdirection to acquire reliable information. A significant amount of deception occurs between romantic and relational partners.

Types

Deception includes several types of communications or omissions that serve to distort or omit the complete truth. Deception itself is intentionally managing verbal and/or nonverbal messages so that the message receiver will believe in a way that the message sender knows is false. Intent is critical with regard to deception. Intent differentiates between deception and an honest mistake. The Interpersonal Deception Theory explores the interrelation between communicative context and sender and receiver cognitions and behaviors in deceptive exchanges.

The five primary forms of deception are:

1. **Lies:** *making up information or giving information that is the opposite or very different from the truth.*
2. **Equivocations:** *making an indirect, ambiguous, or contradictory statement.*
3. **Concealments:** *omitting information that is important or relevant to the given context, or engaging in behavior that helps hide relevant information.*
4. **Exaggerations:** *overstatement or stretching the truth to a degree.*
5. **Understatements:** *minimization or downplaying aspects of the truth.*

Motives

There are three primary motivations for deceptions in close relationships.

- **Partner-focused motives:** *using deception to avoid hurting the partner, to help the partner to enhance or maintain his/her self-esteem, to avoid worrying the partner, and to protect the partner's relationship with a third party. Partner-motivated deception can sometimes be viewed as socially polite and relationally beneficial.*
- **Self-focused motives:** *using deception to enhance or protect their self-image, wanting to shield themselves from anger, embarrassment, or criticism. Self-focused deception is generally perceived as a more serious transgression than partner-focused deception because the deceiver is*

acting for selfish reasons rather than for the good of the relationship.

- **Relationship-focused motives**: *using deception to limit relationship harm by avoiding conflict or relational trauma. Relationally motivated deception can be beneficial to a relationship, and other times it can be harmful by further complicating matters.*

Detection

Deception detection between relational partners is extremely difficult, unless a partner tells a blatant or obvious lie or contradicts something the other partner knows to be true. While it is difficult to deceive a partner over a long period of time, deception often occurs in day-to-day conversations between relational partners. Detecting deception is difficult because there are no known completely reliable indicators of deception. Deception, however, places a significant cognitive load on the deceiver. He or she must recall previous statements so that his or her story remains consistent and believable. As a result, deceivers often leak important information both verbally and nonverbally.

Deception and its detection are a complex, fluid, and cognitive process that are based on the context of the message exchange. The Interpersonal Deception Theory posits that interpersonal deception is a dynamic, iterative process of mutual influence between a sender, who manipulates information to depart from the truth, and a receiver, who attempts to establish the validity of the message. A deceiver's actions are interrelated to the message receiver's actions. It is during this exchange that the deceiver will reveal verbal and nonverbal information about deceit. Some research has found that there are some cues that may be correlated with deceptive communication, but scholars frequently disagree about the effectiveness of many of these cues to serve as reliable indicators. Noted deception scholar Aldert Vrij even states that there is no nonverbal behavior that is uniquely associated with deception. As previously stated, a specific behavioral indicator of deception does not exist. There are, however, some nonverbal behaviors that have been found to be correlated with deception. Vrij found that examining a "cluster" of these cues was a significantly more reliable indicator of deception than examining a single cue.

Truth bias

The truth bias significantly impairs the ability of relational partners to detect deception. In term of deception, a truth bias reflects a tendency to judge more messages as truths than lies, independent of their actual veracity. When judging message veracity, the truth bias contributes to an overestimate of the actual number of truths relative to the base rate of actual truths. The truth bias is especially strong within close relationships. People are highly inclined to trust the communications of others and are unlikely to question the relational partner unless faced with a major deviation of behavior that forces a reevaluation. When attempting to detect deceit from a familiar person or relational partner, a large amount of information about the partner is brought to mind. This information essentially overwhelms the

77

receiver's cognitive ability to detect and process any cues to deception. It is somewhat easier to detect deception in strangers, when less information about that person is brought to mind.

Camouflage

The camouflage of a physical object often works by breaking up the visual boundary of that object. This usually involves coloring the camouflaged object with the same colors as the background against which the object will be hidden. In the realm of deceptive half-truths camouflage is realized by 'hiding' some of the truths.

Disguise

A disguise is an appearance to create the impression of being somebody or something else; for a well-known person this is also called incognito. Passing involves more than mere dress and can include hiding one's real manner of speech.

Example:

- *The fictional Sherlock Holmes often disguised himself as somebody else to avoid being recognized.*

In a more abstract sense, 'disguise' may refer to the act of disguising the nature of a particular proposal in order to hide an unpopular motivation or effect associated with that proposal. This is a form of political spin or propaganda. See also: **rationalization** *and* **transfer** *within the techniques of propaganda generation.*

Example:

- *Depicting an act of war as a "peace" mission.*

Dazzle
Example:

- *The defensive mechanisms of most octopuses to eject black ink in a large cloud to aid in escape from predators.*

Simulation

Simulation consists of exhibiting false information. There are three simulation techniques: mimicry (copying another model), fabrication (making up a new model), and distraction (offering an alternative model)

Mimicry

In the biological world, mimicry involves unconscious deception by similarity to another organism, or to a natural object. Animals for example may deceive predators or prey by visual, auditory or other means.

Fabrication

To make something that in reality is not what it appears to be. For example, in World War II, it was common for the Allies to use hollow tanks made out of cardboard to fool German reconnaissance planes into thinking a large armor unit was on the move in one area while the real tanks were well hidden and on the move in a location far from the fabricated "dummy" tanks.

Distraction

To get someone's attention from the truth by offering bait or something else more tempting to divert attention away from the object being concealed. For example, a security company publicly announces that it will ship a large gold shipment down one route, while in reality take a different route.

In social research

Some methodologies in social research, especially in psychology involve deception. The researchers purposely mislead or misinform the participants about the true nature of the experiment.

In an experiment conducted by Stanley Milgram in 1963 the researchers told participants that they would be participating in a scientific study of memory and learning. In reality the study looked at the participants' willingness to obey commands, even when that involved inflicting pain upon another person. After the study, the subjects were informed of the true nature of the study, and steps were taken in order to ensure that the subjects left in a state of well being.

Use of deception raises many problems of research ethics and it is strictly regulated by professional bodies such as the American Psychological Association.

In psychological research

Psychological research often needs to deceive the subjects as to its actual purpose. The rationale for such deception is that humans are sensitive to how they appear to others (and to themselves) and this self-consciousness might interfere with or distort from how they actually behave outside of a research context (where they would not feel they were being scrutinized). For example, if a psychologist is interested in learning the conditions under which students cheat on tests, directly asking them, "how often do you cheat?," might result in a high percent of "socially desirable" answers and the researcher would in any case be unable to verify the accuracy of these responses. In general, then, when it is unfeasible or naive to simply ask people directly why or how often they do what they do, researchers turn to the use of deception to distract their participants from the true behavior of interest. So, for example, in a study of cheating, the participants may be told that the study has to do with how intuitive they are. During the process they might be given the opportunity to look at (secretly, they think) another participant's [presumably highly intuitively correct] answers before handing in their own. At the conclusion of this or any research involving deception, all participants must be told of the true nature of the study and why deception was necessary (this is called debriefing). Moreover, it is customary to offer to provide a summary *of the results to all participants at the conclusion of the research.*

Though commonly used and allowed by the ethical guidelines of the American Psychological Association, there has been debate about whether or not the use of deception should be permitted in psychological research experiments.

Those against deception object to the ethical and methodological issues involved in its use. Dresser (1981) notes that, ethically, researchers are only to use subjects in an experiment after the subject has given informed consent. However, because of its very nature, a researcher conducting a deception experiment cannot reveal its true purpose to the subject, thereby making any consent given by a subject misinformed (p. 3). Baumrind (1964), criticizing the use of deception in the Milgram (1963) obedience experiment, argues that deception experiments inappropriately take advantage of the implicit trust and obedience given by the subject when the subject volunteers to participate (p. 421).

From a practical perspective, there are also methodological objections to deception. Ortmann and Hertwig (1998) note that "deception can strongly affect the reputation of individual labs and the profession, thus contaminating the participant pool" (p. 806). If the subjects in the experiment are suspicious of the researcher, they are unlikely to behave as they normally would, and the researcher's control of the experiment is then compromised (p. 807).

Those who do not object to the use of deception note that there is always a constant struggle in balancing "the need for conducting research that may solve social problems and the necessity for preserving the dignity and rights of the research participant" (Christensen, 1988, p. 670). They also note that, in some cases, using deception is the only way to obtain certain kinds of information, and that prohibiting all deception in research would "have the egregious consequence of preventing researchers from carrying out a wide range of important studies" (Kimmel, 1998, p. 805).

Additionally, findings suggest that deception is not harmful to subjects. Christensen's (1988) review of the literature found "that research participants do not perceive that they are harmed and do not seem to mind being misled" (p. 668). Furthermore, those participating in experiments involving deception "reported having enjoyed the experience more and perceived more educational benefit" than those who participated in non-deceptive experiments (p. 668).

Lastly, it has also been suggested that an unpleasant treatment used in a deception study or the unpleasant implications of the outcome of a deception study may be the underlying reason that a study using deception is perceived as unethical in nature, rather than the actual deception itself (Broder, 1998, p. 806; Christensen, 1988, p. 671).

In philosophy

Deception is a recurring theme in modern philosophy. In 1641 Descartes published his meditations, in which he introduced the notion of the Deus deceptor, a posited being capable of deceiving the thinking ego about reality. The notion was used as part of his hyperbolic doubt, wherein one decides to doubt everything there is to doubt. The Deus deceptor is a mainstay of so-called skeptical arguments, which purport to put into question our knowledge of reality. The punch of the argument is that all we know might be wrong, since we might be deceived. Stanley Cavell has argued that all skepticism has its root in this fear of deception.

*****

It is interesting to note the article's five primary forms of deception:

> *Lies: making up information or giving information that is the opposite or very different from the truth.*

> *Equivocations: making an indirect, ambiguous, or contradictory statement.*

> *Concealments: omitting information that is important or relevant to the given context, or engaging in behavior that helps hide relevant information.*

> *Exaggerations: overstatement or stretching the truth to a degree.*

Understatements: *minimization or downplaying aspects of the truth.*

What makes it most interesting is that it mixes very recognizable wrongs with some okay stuff too. I mean we all exaggerate and equivocate, right? Is there really any harm in these? Here is where you begin to slip. When you rationalize a wrong into becoming an "okay" or a right then you have begun the downward spiral into the pit of depravity. WRONG is always wrong and never right.

Another interesting aspect to this article is how it defines motive

There are three primary motivations for deceptions in close relationships.

- *Partner-focused motives: using deception to avoid hurting the partner, to help the partner to enhance or maintain his/her self-esteem, to avoid worrying the partner, and to protect the partner's relationship with a third party. Partner-motivated deception can sometimes be viewed as socially polite and relationally beneficial.*
- *Self-focused motives: using deception to enhance or protect their self-image, wanting to shield themselves from anger, embarrassment, or criticism. Self-focused deception is generally perceived as a more serious transgression than partner-focused deception because the deceiver is acting for selfish reasons rather than for the good of the relationship.*

85

- ***Relationship-focused motives****: using deception to limit relationship harm by avoiding conflict or relational trauma. Relationally motivated deception can be beneficial to a relationship, and other times it can be harmful by further complicating matters.*

Again, even the article is using excuses, i. e *"using deception to avoid hurting the partner, to help the partner to enhance or maintain his/her self-esteem, to avoid worrying the partner, and to protect the partner's relationship with a third party"* to justify deception.

It continues, *"using deception to enhance or protect their self-image, wanting to shield themselves from anger, embarrassment, or criticism."* Again, using excuses to justify deception.

This is my favorite, *"using deception to limit relationship harm by avoiding conflict or relational trauma. Relationally motivated deception can be beneficial to a relationship, and other times it can be harmful by further complicating matters."* Oh really?

Are you getting the impression that the article itself is deceiving you? I think in these past chapters you have received a good understanding of exactly what lies, cheating and deception truly are so now let's concentrate on how to become an honest person and correct these problems.

Chapter 6 – How to Become an Honest Person

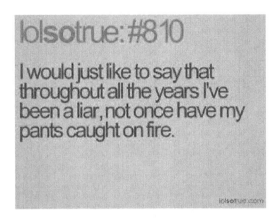

lolsotrue: #810

I would just like to say that throughout all the years I've been a liar, not once have my pants caught on fire.

lolsotrue.com

Honest criticism means nothing: what one wants is
unrestrained passion, fire for fire.
Henry Miller

You have all heard the adage, "Honesty is the best policy." Well, is it? Do you truly believe this? I want to share an article with you and as always I will throw in my 2-cents afterwards.

How to Be Honest

Edited by Jared C., Martyn P, Krystle, Nicole Willson and 52 others

It's been said that honesty is the best policy. It sounds like the simplest thing in the world, but being truly honest with others and with yourself can be a real challenge. Political correctness, being sensitive of other people's feelings, and facing uncomfortable truths about yourself usually requires lots of patience, vigilance and hard work.

Steps

1. **Understand the workings of dishonesty.** *Most of us learned to be dishonest as children. The process often began with the realization that different behaviors result in different outcomes. For example, saying certain things (or not saying certain things) garnered desirable approval and praise, or the undesirable disapproval and censure, if not punishment. Indulgence in dishonest behavior to get desired results was just a small step away. With time the thought processes behind such actions get so entrenched in our subconscious mind that one is not even aware of them. A time comes when one loses the capacity to know when and where to draw the line and how negatively does dishonesty affect our lives (see Warnings below). Dishonesty often becomes a tool to:*
   - *Pretend that there is nothing wrong with us.*
   - *Shift blame to others.*
   - *Avoid embarrassment.*
   - *Distract ourselves.*
   - *Minimize conflict.*
   - *Avoid responsibility or work.*
2. **Fess up.** *Be willing to address issues where you have been less than honest in the past, whether you took a cookie and then denied it, or blatantly lied about whose fault an automobile accident*

88

was. While reviewing your past transgressions can create discomfort and guilt, recognizing where you have been dishonest in the past can help you identify patterns and stop them from continuing.

- o *If you feel guilty for having been dishonest in the past, apologize to the person you lied to and/or find a creative way to make things right. For example, if you kept money that you knew wasn't yours and didn't make a good faith effort to return it to its owner, make an effort to locate the owner and return an equivalent or greater amount or, if you cannot locate the owner after trying, make a donation to charity for an equivalent or greater amount. If you've lied to a person who plays an important role in your life (a significant other, relative, or friend) the best (but most difficult) thing to do is to come clean.*

- o *List the areas where you may have a weakness. It may be as simple as a tendency to make up excuses for failures, or as complicated as a penchant for stealing. Remember that dishonesty is rooted in fear, so you must look for and face those fears. By listing areas where you have a problem, and then working to deal with them, you can consciously battle these habits. If you find yourself lying because you fear disapproval from someone, for example, perhaps you need to learn how to stop being a people pleaser and be yourself. Most importantly, admit your errors so that you can forgive yourself and use those experiences to reinforce your determination to do better. You can't fix what you don't acknowledge as a problem.*

3. **Think honestly**. *This may sound silly, but if you don't think honestly, you won't BE honest. Prejudices and preconceived ideas can make it difficult to distinguish what the truth really is. Don't take things at face value. When you read, see, or hear something, don't make assumptions. Offer the benefit of the doubt, and be skeptical if necessary. When you make a commitment to communicating and understanding the truth, it can be humbling to realize that most of what we think we know is actually just based on assumptions rather than facts. Keep in mind a Jewish proverb: "What you don't see with your eyes, don't witness with your mouth."*

4. **Practice being honest on the simple things**. *This is especially important in situations where "coloring" the facts would make no difference in the world, which covers a good bit of life (from speaking the truth, to avoiding simple thoughtless acts like picking up someone's pencil or grabbing an apple off the neighbor's tree to snack on without thinking about it). Abraham Lincoln became famous for going to great lengths to return a few cents that did not belong to him, hence the nickname "Honest Abe". By applying honesty to the little things, you will get in the habit of being honest in general.*

90

5. ***Exercise tact***. *We all know that being literally honest can hurt feelings and turn friendships sour. It can also be misinterpreted as criticism or a lack of support. It's very tempting to tell a "white lie" when dealing with sensitive loved ones (especially children), but you can still be honest by being creative in how you express the truth.*

   o *Emphasize the positive. Shift the focus away from what, in all honesty, you think is negative. Instead of saying "No, I don't think you look good in those pants" say "They're not as flattering as the black dress—that dress really looks amazing on you. Have you tried it on with those stockings you wore to my cousin's wedding last year?"*

   o *You have the right to remain silent. If you're pushed into a corner and don't know how to respond, say "Can we talk about this another time?" or "I really don't feel comfortable talking about this. You should really address this with..." Don't say "I don't know" if you really do know— it can come back to bite you in the rear later on. The person might catch on and realize that you know something, and they might get pushy. Repeat yourself and leave the conversation as quickly as possible.*

   o *When all else fails, be honest—but gently. Wrap the potentially hurtful truth in appreciation, praise, and, if applicable, affection.*

91

6. *Find a balance between full disclosure and privacy.* *Just because you're honest doesn't mean you have to air out all of your (or anybody else's) business. There are some things that we don't talk about because it's not information that the person asking may be entitled to. On the other hand, withholding information that you know should be disclosed is lying by omission. For instance, not telling a romantic partner that you have a child or that you've been married in the past is objectionable by most. Deciding what information a person should or should not know is a personal decision. Just because you believe a person is better off not knowing something doesn't mean you're acting in their best interest by hiding that information. Follow your gut, and put yourself in that person's position: "If I was in their shoes, would I rightfully feel betrayed if this information wasn't shared with me at an appropriate time?"*

7. *Remember that being honest isn't easy.* *At its core, being honest is difficult because it makes us vulnerable. It shows people who we really are and that we make mistakes, which give them a chance to criticize and reject in a more hurtful way than if we'd hidden the truth or lied to begin with. And sometimes, the truth just hurts. But, honesty develops character, as well as credibility and trust, all of which are the building blocks of high self-esteem and healthy relationships. Being honest isn't a goal that you check off a list—it's an ongoing process that will both challenge and benefit you throughout your life. Nothing is as liberating as having nothing to hide.*

Tips

- *For most people, keeping secrets intended to benefit someone is not considered dishonest, as long as you're confident that the person you're keeping the secret from will completely understand when they find out. Still, it's a fuzzy line determining which secrets are dishonest—keeping a surprise birthday party under wraps is one thing; not telling a child that they are adopted or that their pet has died is trickier, and will require a personal sorting of ethics.*
- *Some may find it helps to keep track of your statements to others in written form (a journal or chart of some sort). This can help you to see how many times you are honest and how many times you are dishonest. Learn from these experiences. Having a record of past situations where you were dishonest can help you to consider what can you do better in future situations. Visualize how it will be if you are honest and then let move forward confidently!*
- *We make judgments, assumptions and theories every day, but in order to be honest, it's important for us to acknowledge them as what they are: ideas about what the truth might be, not the hard truth itself. When you make a statement, try to add the phrase "In my experience..." or "Personally, I've observed that..." at the beginning, or end it with "...but that's just my observation/experience that might not be how things are everywhere". For example: "In my experience, people who have physically demanding jobs tend to be more fit than those in office jobs, but that's just my own*

93

observation. That might not be how things are everywhere." It lets people know that you are making an observation that is limited to your situation, instead of making a blanket statement (i.e. stereotype or generalization) that isn't true.

- *Keep these words of wisdom in mind:*

  - *"Never do something you will have to lie about later. If you have to lie about it, you shouldn't be doing it."*
  - *"Son, always tell the truth. Then you'll never have to remember what you said the last time." Sam Rayburn (1882 - 1961), quoted Washingtonian, November 1978*
  - *"A half truth is a whole lie." Yiddish Proverb*
  - *"Truth fears no questions." Unknown*
  - *"The cruelest lies are often told in silence." Adlai Stevenson*
  - *"Oh what a tangled web we weave, When first we practice to deceive" Sir Walter Scott*

- *If someone pressures you into telling the truth about something you did, say something along the lines of "I did it without thinking. I was wrong to do so. But I know I made a mistake, so I will be better now! Please give me another chance to show you I didn't mean it and that I can be a good friend".*

- *Being honest really can be truly hard, but to be a stronger person we need to except that before we become honest we need to put all our mistakes out on the table. There for you can answer their questions about you're fowl long mistakes.*

Warnings

- *Be wary when someone tells you something in confidence, and you know in your gut that you should share that information with someone else (knowledge of a crime, a lie, or a harmful act against another). This puts you in a difficult position, especially when the truth eventually comes out and the person affected by it finds out you knew all along. If someone starts off a sentence with "Don't tell so-and-so about this, okay?" be prepared to offer your own disclaimer: "If it's something that I'd want to know about if I was in their shoes, please don't tell me. I don't want to be responsible for keeping anyone's secrets but my own."*
- *Be conscious of groups of peers or friends who may sway you to "stray" from your choice to stay on the "straight and narrow". Like any bad habit, you may be pressured to regress if you choose to hang around people who don't have integrity and don't cherish honesty. You don't have to automatically find new, more truthful friends, but be aware of your vulnerability to temptation if you continue associations with overtly dishonest people.*
- *If you find that you cannot control your lying, there may be emotional issues at work that are beyond the scope of this article. Consider meeting with a counselor or other professional who can*

help you work through those issues over the long term. It may be that dishonesty is a habit that you've set for your entire life, and it will take a good deal of introspection and work to unravel that pattern.

- *Dishonesty has many negative consequences. They are often not immediate or noticeable; they usually build up over time until they hit us like a brick wall, at which point it may be difficult to see how dishonesty has played a role in unhappiness. Consequences may include:*
  - *Becoming numb to our own feelings if we hide them for a long enough time*
  - *Becoming deeply confused about what we actually want*
  - *Making a bad situation worse*
  - *Not being prepared to face the consequences of our decisions and the reality of our situation, thus getting more hurt by it in the end*
  - *Being haunted by guilt and fear that your dishonesty will be discovered*
  - *An emotional state that can be best described as a "heavy heart"*

*****

Okay, in our law enforcement seminars where we teach trained observation an interrogation tactics one thing that stands out is this: a liar always scripts their responses so by asking numerous questions, you can trip them up so that they simply cannot remember where they left off in the script.

Somebody telling the truth doesn't have a script so when you ask them questions they can easily pick up where they left off.

This is why the police ask you so many questions – one right after another – to see if you are lying or not.

Truth needs no companion; it stands alone and is the utmost form of honesty. Becoming a truthful person runs deep within your soul. It is a direct result of your character. Becoming honest means changing a good many things about yourself. If you have the proper mindset then you will succeed.

Now, allow me to sum it all up for you…

Chapter 7 – Summary & Conclusions

Throughout this book I have been teaching leis, cheating and deception but more importantly, the causes of this wrongful behavior and that this condition goes deeper than what appears on the surface.

In Chapter 1, this chapter was designed to teach you the science behind the condition; to get you to understand why you do the things you do and then the necessary steps to correct any form of behavior/conduct/action that stems from the subconscious mind.

In Chapter 2, my purpose was to define the gain in lying, cheating and deception for if there is no gain then it is all in vain. But the gain is usually in the form of "perceived" gain and not real gain...a very big difference.

In Chapter 3, I defined why people lie. What causes people to tell untruths and why do they find it necessary to do this.

In Chapter 4, I continued in defining cheating. When a person thinks of cheating, what most often comes to mind is infidelity or cheating on a spouse or mate. But cheating goes much deeper than this and I provided a plethora of causes and results of cheating.

In Chapter 5, I defined the act of deception in general and this is the mother of all forms of lying and cheating. I used an article that actually rationalized deception and used this article to demonstrate that once a person engages in any form of rationalization of any wrong, it is the beginning of the spiral down into depravity.

In Chapter 5, I expanded on how to become an honest person and this is to be used with how to change the subconscious mind in Chapter 1. With the proper mindset, a person can overcome virtually anything by changing the subconscious mind.

I hope you enjoyed my book. Now I have a special gift for you. Read on...

I Have a Special Gift for My Readers

I appreciate my readers for without them I am just another author attempting to make a difference. If my book has made a favorable impression please leave me an honest review. Thank you in advance for you participation.

My readers and I have in common a passion for the written word as well as the desire to learn and grow from books.

My special offer to you is a massive ebook library that I have compiled over the years. It contains hundreds of fiction and non-fiction ebooks in Adobe Acrobat PDF format as well as the Greek classics and old literary classics too.

In fact, this library is so massive to completely download the entire library will require over 5 GBs open on your desktop.

Use the link below and scan all of the ebooks in the library. You can select the ebooks you want individually or download the entire library.

The link below does not expire after a given time period so you are free to return for more books rather than clog your desktop. And feel free to give the link to your friends who enjoy reading too.

I thank you for reading my book and hope if you are pleased that you will leave me an honest review so that I can improve my work and or write books that appeal to your interests.

Okay, here is the link…

http://tinyurl.com/special-readers-promo

PS: If you wish to reach me personally for any reason you may simply write to mailto:support@epubwealth.com.

I answer all of my emails so rest assured I will respond.

Meet the Author

Dr. Leland Benton is Director of Applied Web Info, a holding company for ePubWealth.com, a leading ePublisher company based in Utah. With over 21,000 resellers in over 22-countries, ePubWealth.com is a leader in ePublishing, book promotion, and ebook marketing.

As the creator and author of "The ePubWealth Program," Leland teaches up-and-coming authors the ins-and-outs of today's ePublishing world. He has assisted hundreds of authors make it big in the ePublishing world.

Leland also created a series of external book promotion programs and teaches authors how to promote their books using external marketing sources.

Leland is also the Managing Director of Applied Mind Sciences, the company's mind research unit and Chief Forensics Investigator for the company's ForensicsNation unit. He is active in privacy rights through the company's PrivacyNations unit and is an expert in survival planning and disaster relief through the company's SurvivalNations unit.

Leland resides in Southern Utah.

Visit some of his websites
http://appliedmindsciences.com/
http://appliedwebinfo.com/
http://BoolbuilderPLUS.com
http://embarrassingproblemsfix.com/
http://www.epubwealth.com/

http://forensicsnation.com/
http://neternatives.com/
http://privacynations.com/
http://survivalnations.com/
http://thebentonkitchen.com
http://theolegions.org

Made in the USA
San Bernardino, CA
10 November 2016